Skeleton
Coloring Book
For Adults

This Book Belongs To

____

All Illustrations Are Hand Drawn

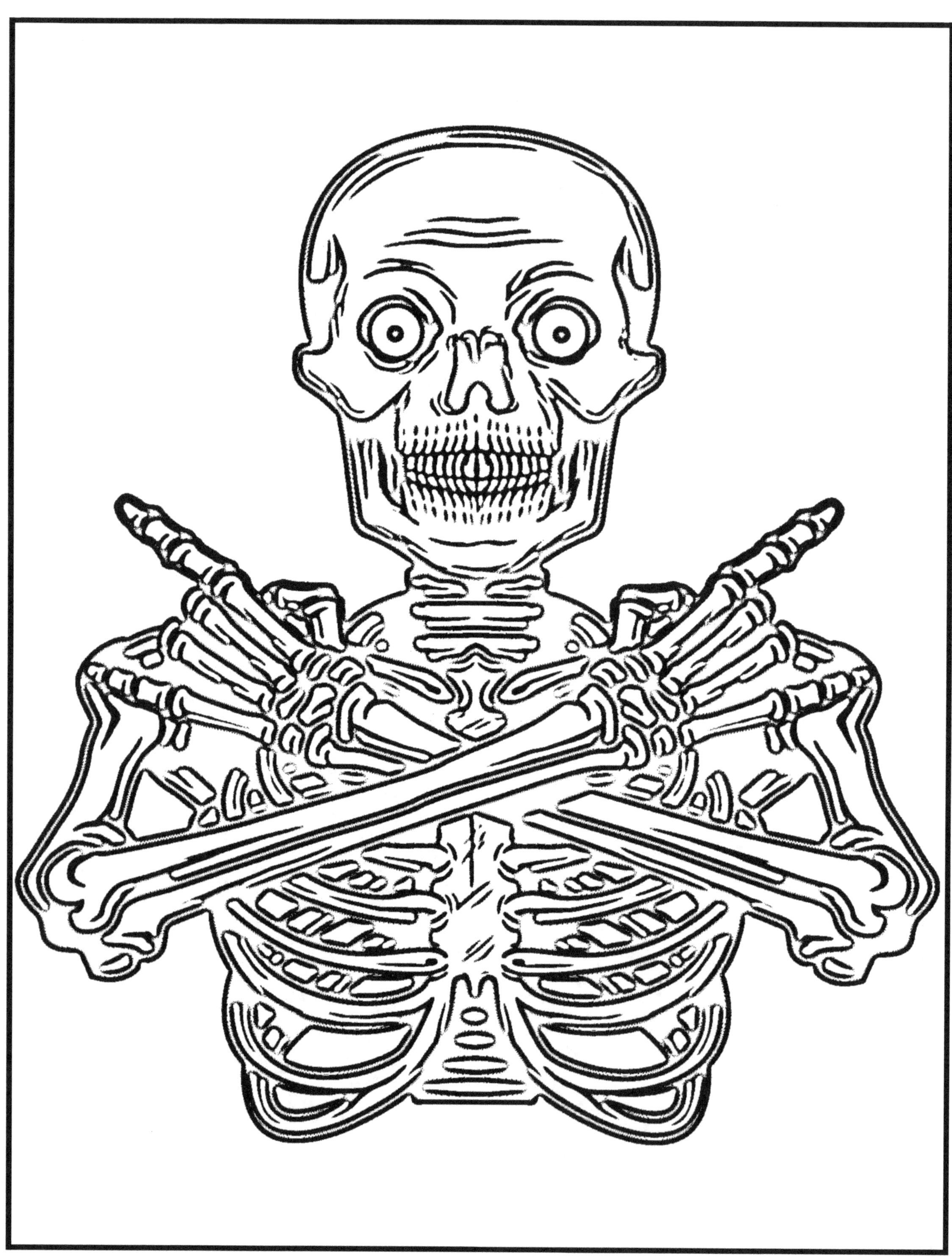

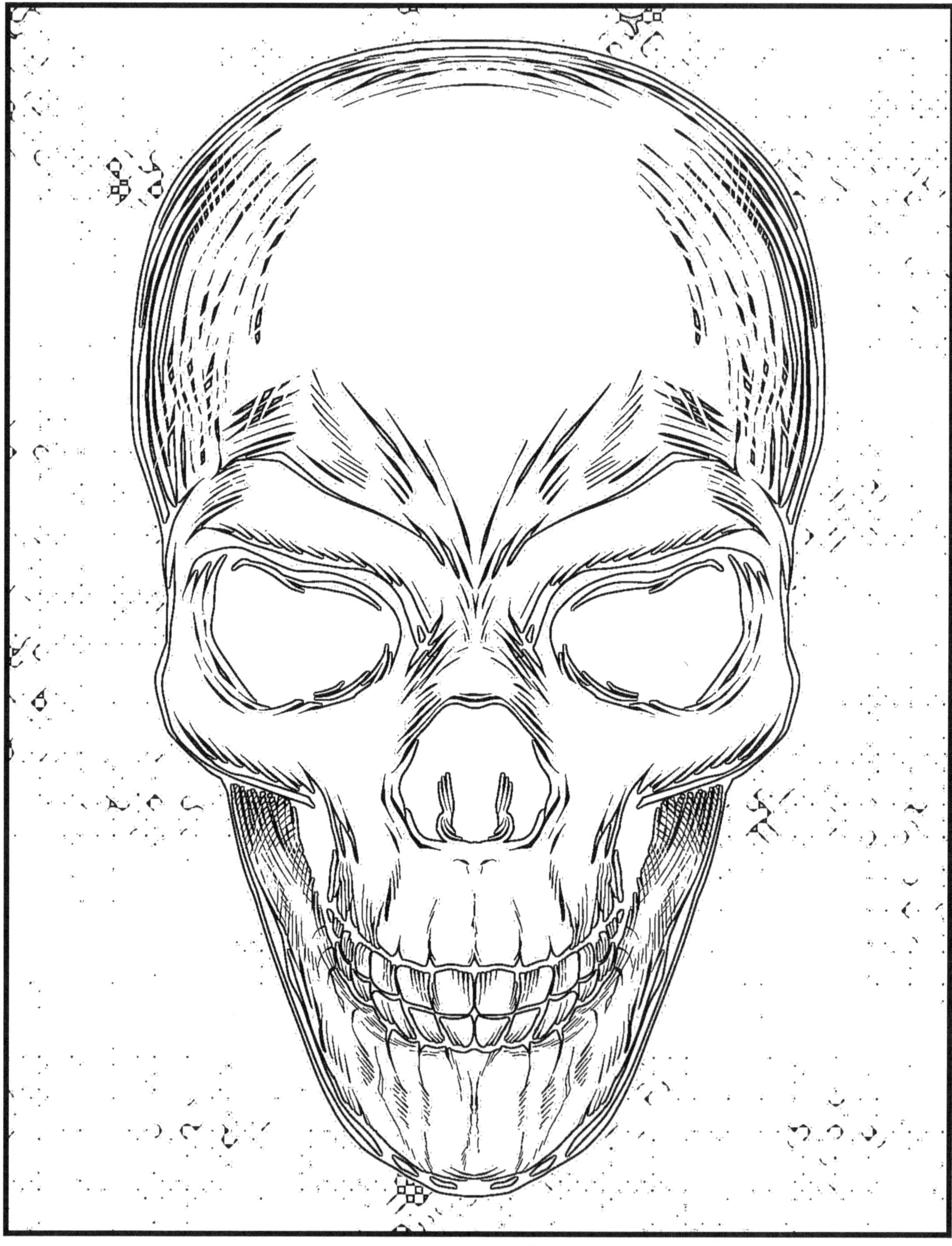

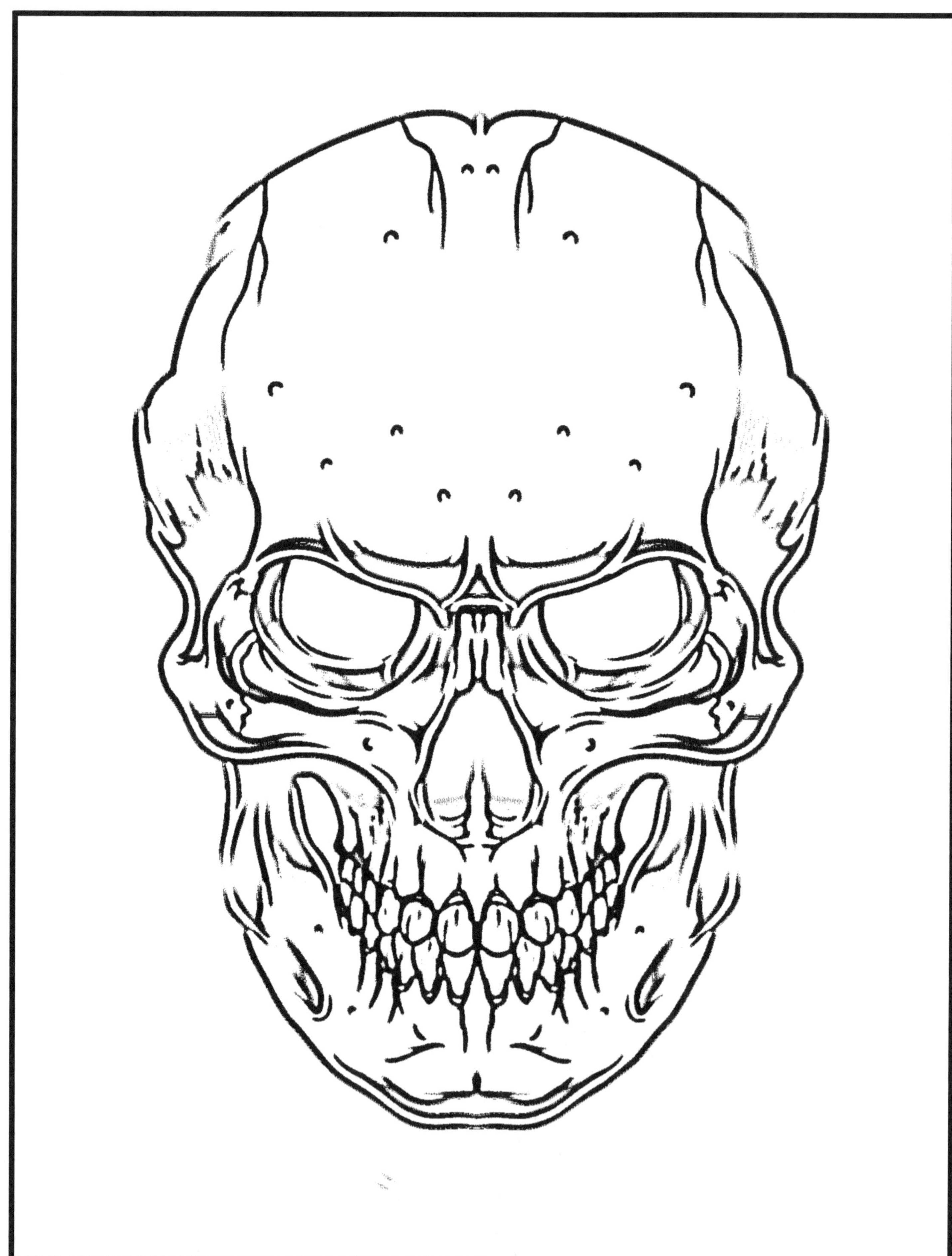

SKULL SINGER

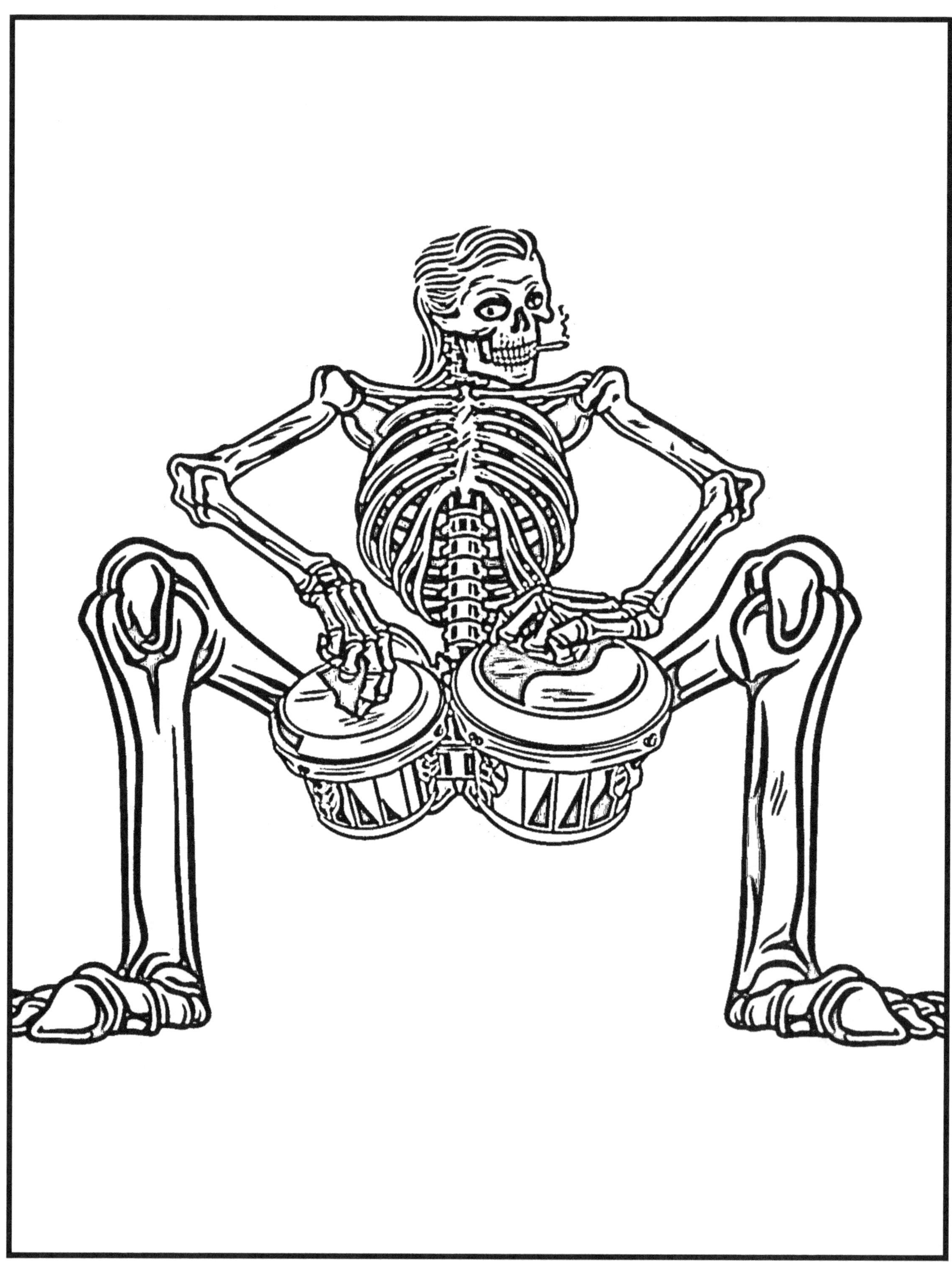

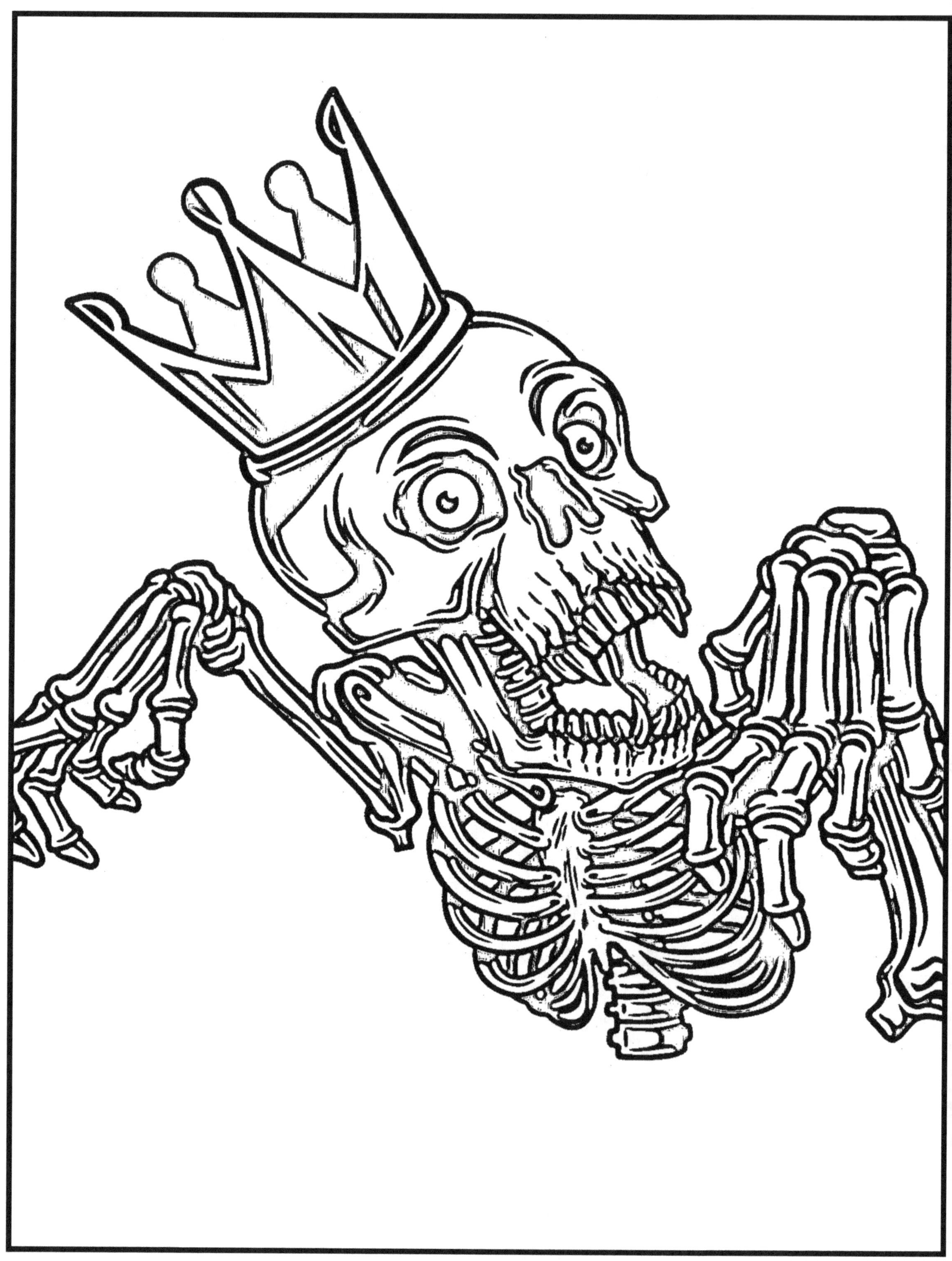

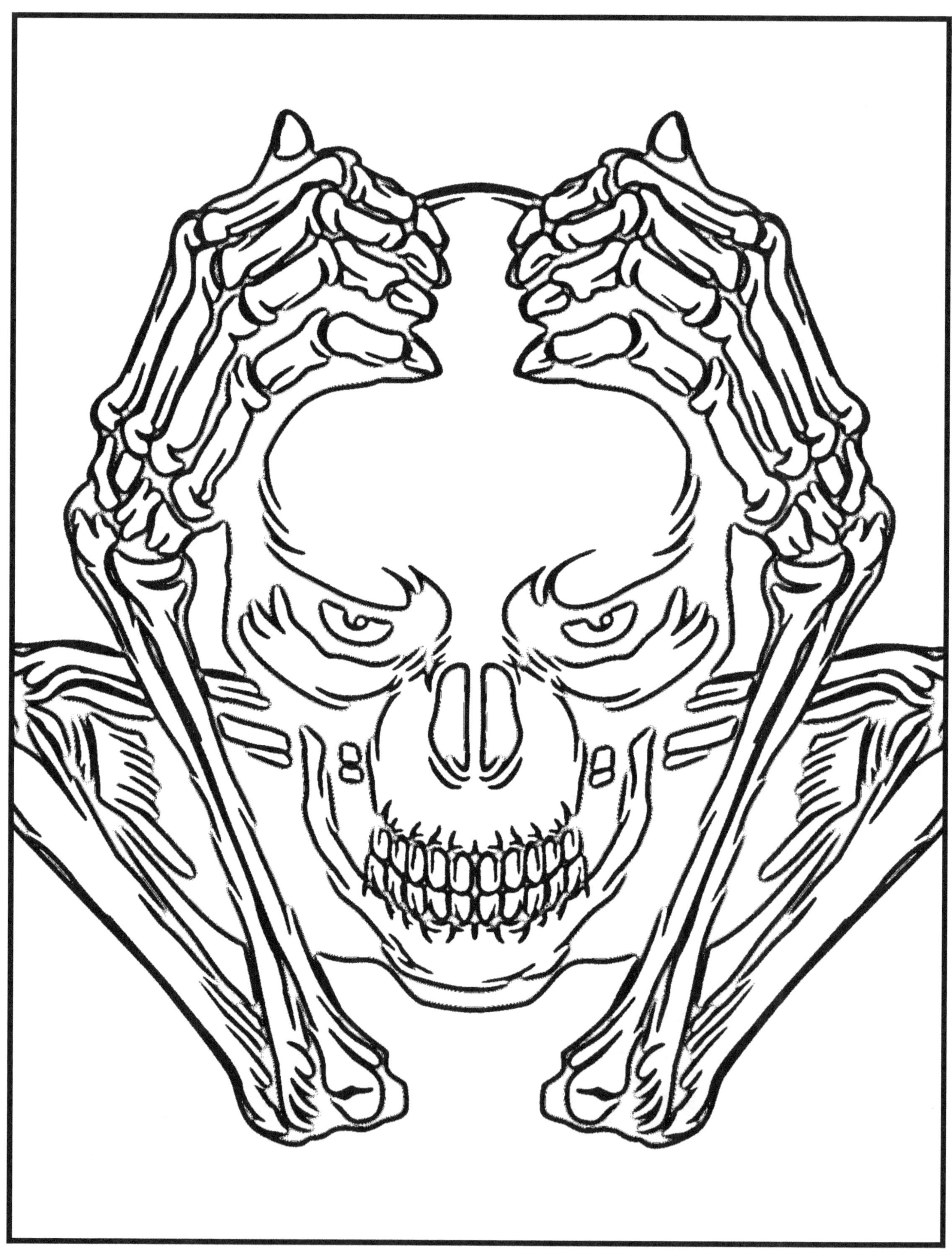

GRIM REAPER

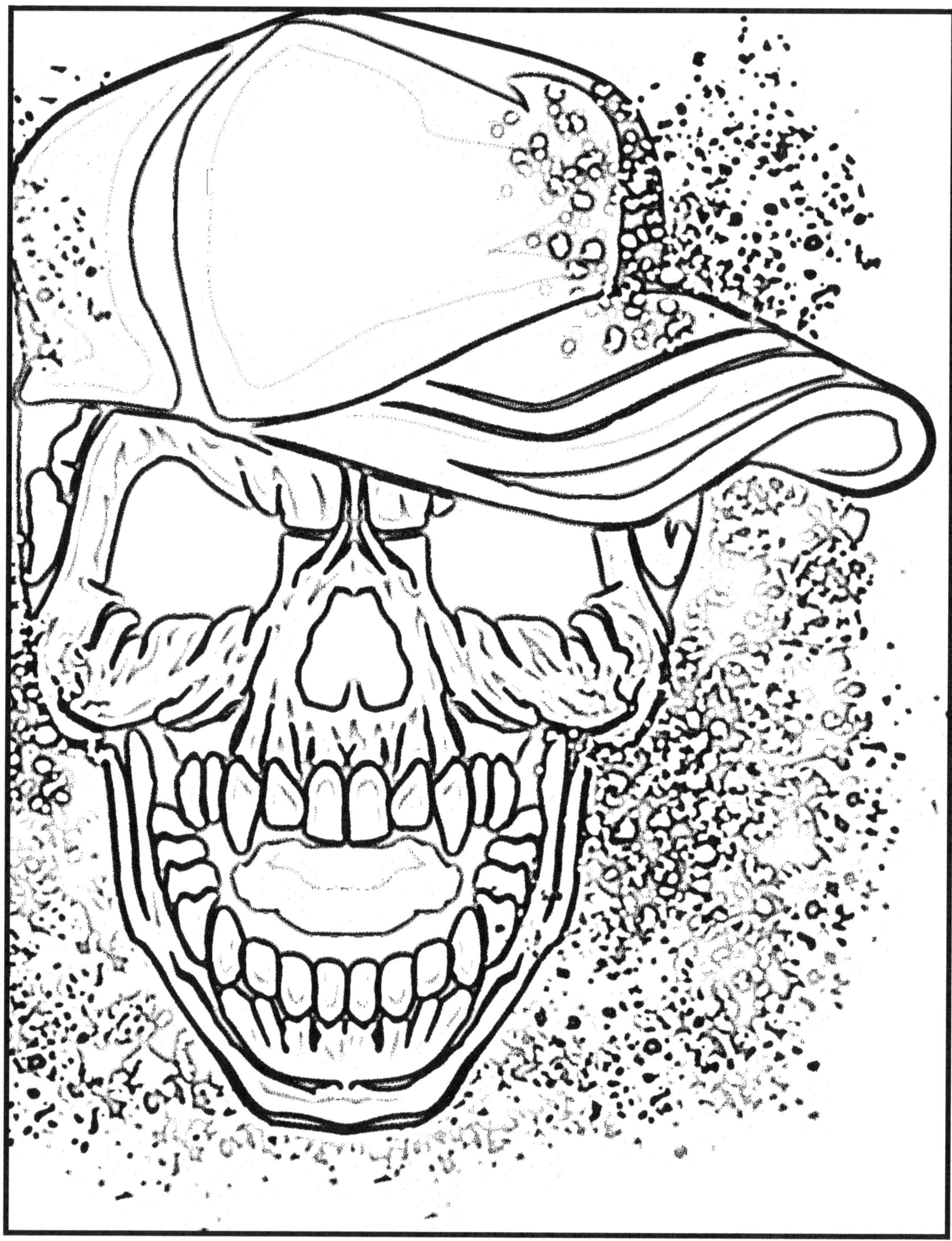

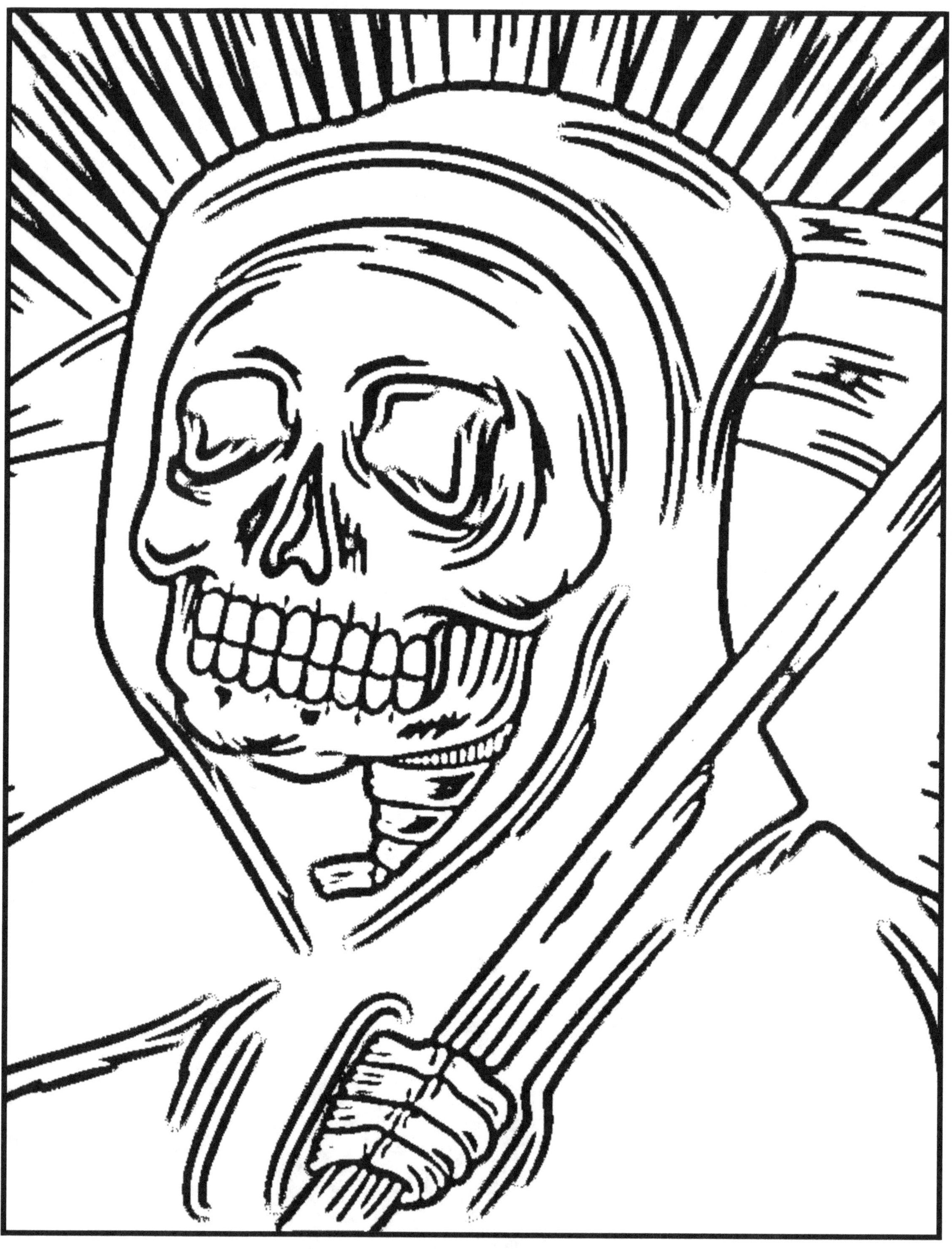

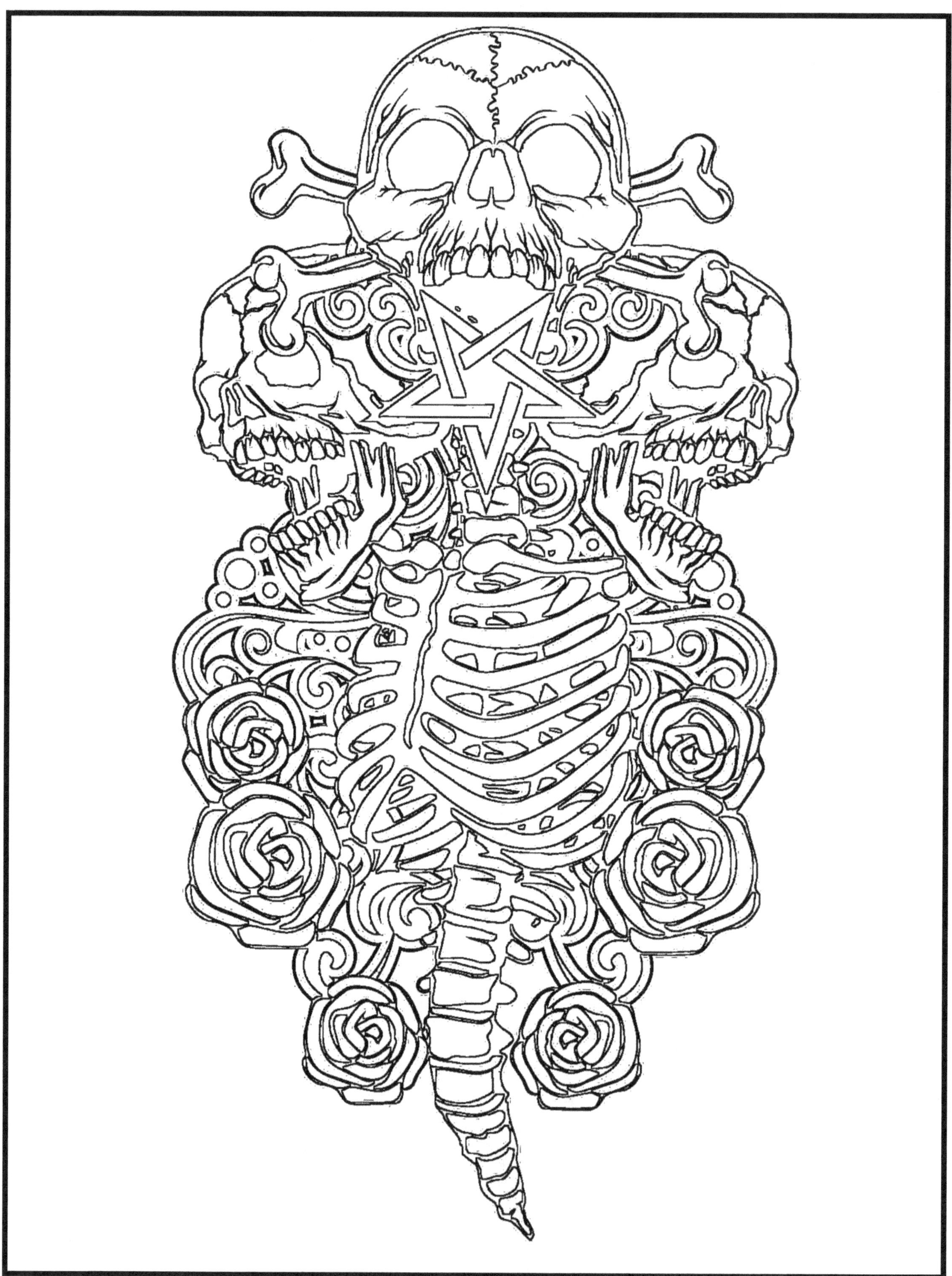